1

© Knowledge Books and Software

My name is Mark Tirris. I am from a large family and I have six siblings. My mother is Aboriginal and her grandfather is from the Wiradjuri people of South West New South Wales. My father is Greek, so this means that I'm both Aboriginal and Greek. My family is multicultural and we share many things across these two cultures.

3

Many Aboriginal families are like mine. I like to be both Aboriginal and Greek. Aboriginal people can look different to each other. We are still Aboriginal even though my family doesn't all look the same. We like being Aboriginal and doing things together to celebrate our Aboriginal heritage.

5

My family likes to visit our relatives down South. We go on big road trips and drive for hours. The children get very tired and sleep in the car. We visit our relatives when someone has had a baby, or a wedding, or when someone has died. We like to visit our relatives even though they live far away. This way we stay close to our relatives in our heart.

When my relatives visit me, we have lots of fun. All the children go swimming and play board games. We also dance, and draw, and eat lots of yummy food. We all take turns cooking the meals and sharing the food. The uncles and aunties and grandparents, tell the kids stories about life, and about being Aboriginal. One of the uncles plays the didgeridoo, and shows the kids how to make clap sticks and boomerangs. The kids love learning how to make these special Aboriginal instruments and tools.

One of the activities I like to do when the children visit is carving. We select a branch off a tree. The branch is cut, and the bark is pulled off the branch. We then take the branch, and cut it into smaller pieces. These pieces are used to make clap sticks. My uncle teaches the children to use the clap sticks and dance. The children learn the dance of the sea eagle, the emu and the kangaroo.

11

I am very close to my siblings, even now that I'm older. I am the middle child. Growing up, we used to sometimes get angry with each other. We would try to beat each other at sports. We were very competitive. Sometimes we would also get hurt. We would learn things from getting hurt. Now that we're older, we don't see each other as much. However, when we do catch up, we talk lots and give each other hugs. We will always be brothers, no matter how far away from one another we are.

13

I have a large extended family. They live in many different places. Some live close to the beach. Some live in big cities, and some live near the bush. My relatives do many different things. Some have jobs and some study. Some take care of their children. Some are sick and cannot work or study. Aboriginal people can live in many different places. It doesn't matter where they live. They are still Aboriginal and they can still practise their culture anywhere.

15

Sometimes we have someone die in my family. When someone dies we call it 'sorry business'. When someone dies, all my relatives come together to be sad. We cry and say goodbye to the person that died. We talk to each other and remember the good times from the past. It can be very expensive to have a funeral. Sometimes the whole family needs to contribute to help pay for it. Sorry business is very important to my Aboriginal family.

17

Now that I am an adult I have my own children and family. I have two sons, two and four years old. They like to learn about being Aboriginal. I play with them and show them how to run, jump, climb and swim. I show them how to play the didgeridoo and how to dance. We do drawings and paintings of animals in Aboriginal style. We visit other Aboriginal kids in the park and talk and play with them. As they get older they will learn more about their Aboriginal family and their culture. One day they will be adults and may have children. Then they can teach Aboriginal culture to their children too.

My family keeps growing. Every year there are more babies born. Every year someone gets married. The new person's family is joined to our family. As my family grows, more different cultures merge with our family. Some of my family have relatives in Africa and the Middle East. Some of my family have married people from Asia. The non-Aboriginal people who come into my family get to learn about our culture. We can all learn about each other and be kind and friendly.

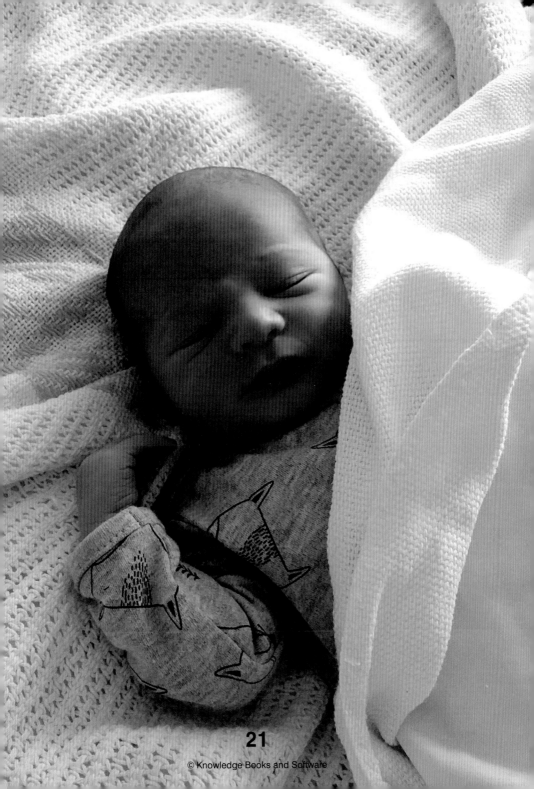

21

My family likes it when we see other Aboriginal people doing good things. We like to see Aboriginal people play sports for the Olympic games. We like seeing Aboriginal people in politics or in business. We like to hear about their success stories. Sometimes we will go to events to see a famous Aboriginal person. We like to support other Aboriginal people and businesses. The past has been hard for many Aboriginal people. If we support each other, we will all be stronger and smarter. We will all have a better future together.

23

Word bank

Tirris

siblings

Aboriginal

grandfather

Wiradjuri

Greek

multicultural

cultures

different

celebrate

heritage

relatives

didgeridoo

boomerangs

special

instruments

competitive

practise

sorry business

remember

expensive

contribute

Africa

Asia

non-Aboriginal

Olympic

politics